GOD'S PURPOSE, GOD'S PLAN, AND
GOD'S USE FOR YOUR LIFE

CAREY GIDRON Sr.

PROMOTED BY BETRAYAL

THE TENACITY TO BE EXCEPTIONAL

Promoted by Betrayal

God's Purpose, God's Plan, and God's Use for Your Life

Carey Gidron, Sr.

ISBN (Print Edition): 978-1-09831-667-9

ISBN (eBook Edition): 978-1-09831-668-6

TABLE OF CONTENTS

AUTHOR'S NOTE

Promoted by Betrayal is not just another book; it is truly a clarion call to all who read it. The hope is that they will discover and access their place on earth. This book is a shared journey of my life; a journey upon which the average person would not desire to embark simply because of the deep hurts and pains that's revealed. Yet I have found that this journey places a demand for humility and submission to God while relinquishing the past to move forward.

As you read this book, I pray that great desires will be born in you and that you will discover God's plan for your life and move forward with the vision and dreams that's within you.

DEDICATION

First and foremost, I would like to dedicate this book to my mother and father, the late *Reverend John Gidron* and *Mrs. Brenda Gidron.* Who have been the epitomes of love, happiness, and courage throughout the duration of their earthly existence, two individuals who have empowered me to strive for the success God has bestowed upon and predestined me for.

I also dedicate this book to my wife D. *Michelle Gidron.* To my lovely wife, I would like to say thank you for being the essence of grace and love in my life. I appreciate your continuous courage, support, and strength as it pertains to my every life endeavor. I thank you for the balance that you've created in my life. Thank you for sticking with me through the various changes of seasons in our married life. I love you forever.

I dedicate this book to my five amazing sons: *Carey, Michael, Ethan, Joseph,* and my God-given son *Jermaine.* Thank you all for making life a roller-coaster of happiness, joy, and laughter. I am so happy that God has entrusted me to be the father of some of the greatest minds of this generation. Continue your path of success and happiness, and remember Daddy is always here to love and support you all.

I also dedicate this book to, my Godparents: *the late Dr. Bettye Vassel, Pastor Samuel Sago,* and *Elder Charles "Chuck" Lewis, Barber and Wardell Campbell.* I would like to say thank you to these five amazing individuals for coming into my life. I appreciate you all for not trying to replace my mother and father but being able to fulfill and complete their assignment where I am concerned. I am grateful for the wisdom, love, guidance, and support you all give to me daily.

My Testimony

The youngest son of six children, I was born on December 14, 1976 in Chicago, Illinois to John and Brenda Gidron. Growing up, I soon found out that even though I was a pastor's kid, or P.K., I was neither exempt nor shielded from the hard knocks of life. Holiness was not found as a principle in the household of my extended family. Gangs, drugs, alcohol and jail instead became the lifestyle of many of my family members, based on the choices that they made. Now don't get me wrong, my family was and still is a great family—just not a church-going, shouting, dancing, speaking-in-tongues type of family.

My dad didn't become a preacher until after his mom (my grandma) died. By the age of ten, I had already experienced a life with many obstacles. My life became like David in the bible out of my brothers, I was the one chosen by God. I was able to rise above all the negative forces around me. I became the second generation of Gidron's to preach the Gospel. At ten years old God blessed me and put His hand of favor upon my life to preach His Holy Word. By that time, my life story had already begun to be written; the wall of betrayal, pain and secrets was already built.

I never could have imagined that as a child I would have experienced one of the most life-shattering and soul-shaking experiences of my life—something that would lock me in a box of no return. One that would build a wall not easily destroyed; it was the experience of secret betrayal. I was about eight years old when one of my family members tried to molest me, and not just once but several times. I had no one to help or protect me. This wound grew deeper and deeper, and to this day, it has held its ground in my life. Although I refused to fall victim to the spirit of what my family member tried to put upon me and my life, I still became a victim—not to homosexuality, but to hate.

I have always known that men becoming involved with other men were and always have been wrong, so I was never sexually attracted to another man. However, I became something far more dangerous than one who battles the war of identity crisis; I became the exact opposite. I developed a great deal of hatred for people with that lifestyle.

My hatred ran so deep into the very core of my soul that it controlled my life in every way. If I was preaching the Gospel it was there, if I was out to eat it was there; even if I was at the cleaners it was there!!!—if I saw a gay person, I immediately became disgusted and angry.

The hatred I had toward homosexuals was bad and so out of control, True story I remember one time, I was invited to this church to preach. After I was done, I called for a prayer line. There were two young men who were publicly bound by an alternative lifestyle, and one of them asked me to pray for him. He said that he really wanted to be free, and he believed that if I prayed for him God would set him free. I agreed to pray for him; however, I didn't. After service was over, one of my assistants asked why I skipped over him, and I just shrugged it off like I forgot. The truth was that I hated homosexuals and I just could not find it within myself to pray for them. After all, who prayed for me while I was being betrayed by the very one who should have been protecting me—in my own family? I was full of hatred, hatred that I could not explain.

Many days in my childhood, teens, and well into my adult life, I was left crying on the inside battling a war of hatred in my heart and praying on my knees pleading with God to take away my pain. I did not understand why at such a young age the light of life seemed as if it had been snatched away from me right before my very eyes. For a long time, I found myself smiling and laughing on the outside as my defense to cover up my secret cries of betrayal on the inside. I was left naked, left in the deep fears of my mind with no one to cover or protect me from the enemy within.

Every day of my life I questioned myself about how to eliminate this demon of hatred inside me, knowing that if I didn't get free, I would never be right in my mind or my life. I knew that there was a way out; I just didn't know how to get there. I couldn't take it anymore. I was crying out to the Lord, asking Him to clothe my soul. I was left here naked and in despair with no one to help me. I pleaded for God to give me new life—to let me live again. I'd grown tired of being alone in my room at night, having nightmares of ending it all, and saying to myself, "Enough is enough."

I wanted it to end. I wanted to tell my mom and dad or find someone I could confide in, but I couldn't. I just couldn't because I grew up in a different kind of home; the kind of home where the rule of what goes on in this house stays in this house. It was some kind of life, not knowing who you could talk to or trust. After all, I was just a little kid. I could never come up with the proper reasoning for why this happened to me, *"Then it happen my eyes were open the lord spoke and said Carey you are angry at the wrong people and spirit, the demon that you are fighting is not the demonic force of homosexuality it's the spirit of Child molestation…you see just because a person is gay it doesn't mean that person is a child molester"*…it was at that moment my eyes and outlook open up big time about the gay community and my deliverance started.

"My mom would always say that time heals all wounds, but I say that forgiveness heals all wounds."

Recently I confronted my family member about the pain, anger, hatred, and frustration I felt deep on the inside, asking him what I did to deserve such hurt and pain. Only to find out from the voice of my family member that he was acting out what had been done to him. Wow, talk about a generational curse; but I thank God for the anointing and the spirit of forgiveness. My family member said, "Please forgive me, I'm sorry, I'm not this evil dark person who you may think I am, but I too was left in this cave of darkness, I only acted out what was placed upon my life, and I'm sorry for destroying your life." At that moment I knew that God was real because I asked God to help me get through this and to help me walk into a place of forgiveness and he did. I am grateful that my life is now changed through the power of forgiveness and I am free because of it. Deliverance is real….. Amen

My Testimony,

CHAPTER 1

THE JOURNEY

M y life is like an aircraft that flies into deep dark storms and one of its engines blows, thereby making it necessary for the pilot to find safe landing. To further complicate matters, there are people on board whose lives depend on this injured aircraft. So, if not careful, both the aircraft and the individuals could crash and die.

That's how I feel as a vessel of God writing this book. I am the pilot; the reader is the passenger; my life is the injured aircraft. As you travel this journey with me, you will experience my life-changing experiences, past hurts, open wounds, broken promises, and hidden secrets so buckle up and let's began this journey together.

"Moving forward and accessing God's purpose and plan for your life after a season of public exposure and shame is never as difficult as getting past your hurt and betrayal. It only defines the next level of your life,"

~ **Carey Gidron Sr.** ~ implementing forgiveness becomes necessary if you desire to demonstrate that you are truly ready to be more like God. If you want to prove that you can handle the assignment for your life, then you must stay focus and humble yourself even when things become uncomfortable in order to become who he has called you to be in this life, *Promoted By Betrayal* entails great discomfort and thrusts you into your Ark season, which is when God allows you to go on a journey that will teach you and change your life forever.

One of the stages in this journey is **Uneasiness**. I'm reminded of Genesis 7:16, when God shut Noah in the Ark. He was on board with animals of every kind and had to experience the discomfort of being closed in with his family and the animals. There was no bathroom, no shower—the smell must have been terribly unbearable.

Noah discovered that he had no control of the situation; he realized that only God had total control. Can you imagine what Noah had to be thinking? But like Noah, we must realize that God allows us to experience a small season of tests (adjustments) to see if we can truly handle the actual assignment as well as the level of trust that he puts within us.

The Bible says, "By faith, Noah hears and obeys the voice of God to build this Ark to save his family. By his faith he condemned the world and became heir of the righteousness that is in keeping with faith." (Heb. 11:7.)

This story in the Bible is one of the most catastrophic events of human history—the flood and Ark of Noah. Although it took place thousands of years ago, the story of the flood/Ark have many important lessons for us even today; allow me to share three of them with you now!

1. The boat is for you as well. Don't miss out! I almost missed it!

One day I was traveling to preach out of town, it was my first time going to Greenwood MS This event had been publicized by the pastor who I was preaching for. I was excited. I remember it like it was yesterday. The people came from everywhere...well to make a long story short, I finally got to the airport to realize that my plane was at the gate and it had already boarded and they were at the final boarding call and I was still at the ticket counter with 10 minutes on the clock. It seemed I was not going to make it on this flight. The sad thing is that this flight was a game changer, because it was the last flight out to my destination. I tell you I ran and ran. I had to ask for assistance from the ticket counter to get me through the security check, and by the grace of God I made it on the flight. All of this happened simply because I didn't properly plan. I didn't heed to the travel instruction that said arrive one hour to two hours early. Can you imagine what could have happen if I had missed that flight? So many people would have been disappointed, I would have messed up a good relationship, and the pastor would have lost his money that he spent on the flight and hotel…all because I didn't properly plain my trip. You see, everything was paid for, and all I had to do was be on time. My point is this, people. Everything is paid for. All you have to do is (1) be on time and (2) be in place ready to go.

Remember, "**Early arrival is required.**" Can you imagine how much more terrible it was for those who missed getting on Noah's Ark? There were no last-minute arrivals allowed, no holding the Boat. God had Noah, his family, and the animals get on the Ark SEVEN DAYS EARLY, and then He "shut them in." There were no rain clouds visible when he told them to get in. They got in by faith, when it looked foolish. They sat in the Ark for seven days, with no rain outside (Gen. 7:10). That must have been a faith-trying time! Only eight people made it; millions drowned. They missed out on salvation simply because they thought Noah was foolish. The Bible teaches us: "For God has chosen the foolish of the world to confound the wise, and he has chosen the weak of the world to shame the mighty. But God chose what the world considers nonsense to put wise people to shame. God chose what the world considers weak to put what is strong to shame."

(1 Corinthians 1:27.)

His method today isn't often accepted or popular, but it's still the only way to heaven. If you're going to get into the Ark of safety, you need to get in now before the storm arrives!

2. Plan ahead. It wasn't raining when Noah built the Ark!

God can do anything!

A very interesting feature of this account was that the flood depended on rainfall. AND UP TO THAT MOMENT THERE HAD NEVER BEEN RAIN!

Now if I told you the world would be destroyed by a tidal wave of lemonade (my favorite), you would think I was crazy, because lemonade doesn't exist in the quantities necessary to cause a tidal wave— although we wish it did! For Noah, it wasn't just the uncertainty of building the Ark and all the animals coming to him, but even the means of the destruction had never occurred before! Now we've never seen the rapture. Today we live with a science community that is convinced that such an event like a rapture is impossible. They would have told Noah the same thing. But Noah didn't care if it was impossible, he still believed God and began to make proper preparations. This is a generation that only wants to see signs; they want to wait until they see the sun darkened, the moon "dipped in blood," and the stars exploding out of their orbits before they get right with God.

3. Stay in shape. Biblical history teaches that Noah was 500 when asked to build the Ark.

I can only imagine and dream about what it feels to be 500 years old. You and I can only wonder if Noah, at 500, got tired by three o'clock. Did he have aches and pains? Did his knees squeak? Like today's older men, had he lost his strong muscular shape and gained a potbelly like most?

I'm sure at this age he had worked hard for many years and built up his life's work until he was well pleased. He undoubtedly thought, *it's finally time for me to be able to have a breather and enjoy the latter years of my life.* I've known several people who worked where I work, at the transit authority, which took an early retirement at 48 or 52 years old, and began enjoying a long, calming retirement.

You and I both would say what a shocker, for God to ask 500-year-old Noah to build a vessel with 1.5 million cubic feet capacity, the equivalent of 569 modern railroad cars! The floor space of the Ark was over 101,000 square feet. It was the largest vessel ever built until the late 1800s. Noah had already served God and done God's will for 500 years. Surely that was enough! Surely God could find some young strong energetic person full of life in his 20s or 30s with no wife or children to attend to! Instead, God chose a 500-year-old man who stayed ready and willing even in his old age. So now my question to you is simple: Are you fit and ready? In spite of your assignment and the betrayal you will experience or encounter, are you fit in the spirit?

Spiritually Fit

Noah was not only fit physically, he was also spiritually fit—that is, he maintained a close relationship with God so that he could be instructed, daily, on the details of his enormous task. Noah stayed prayed up, sensitive, full of the Holy Spirit—his mind filled with the thoughts of God, even though he lived in a corrupt and degenerate time of great betrayal, disloyalty, and unfaithfulness. Likewise, if we want to be ready, we must stay spiritually alert and full of God's Word and Spirit. There's no room for experimenting in the world or participating in its ways; the word of God is right; it says, "Wherefore come out from among them, and be ye **separate**, saith the Lord, and touch not the unclean thing; and I will receive you, and will be a Father unto you, and ye shall be my sons and daughters, saith the Lord Almighty" (2 Cor. 6:17-18). People will always find fault with the church and with Christians. Why? Because people aren't perfect and there're always problems. Welcome to the journey!

CHAPTER 2

Unresolved Issues

Personal Betrayal

Have you ever become frustrated, angry, or bitter because of ministry work, or because the things we believe God has called us to do not work out? I am one who has walked in those shoes so many times. I've experienced great betrayal in life, but discovered that in many of those stages, God kept and protected me.

Betrayal is a very vicious thing; dictionary.com, states that it means "to deliver or expose to an enemy by treachery or disloyalty to be unfaithful in guarding, maintaining, or fulfilling." In the word of God, we find many stories of great betrayal. Three come to mind: Joseph and his brothers, Jacob and Esau, and Samson and Delilah. Each story becomes more and more significant and very relevant in today's generation.

As you continue to read this book, I ask that you open your heart and mind to understand the things that make many great leaders who they are today; every great leader must go through trials. Luke 12:48 says, "But he that knew not, and did commit things worthy of stripes, shall be beaten with few stripes. For unto whomsoever much is given, of him shall much be required: and to whom men have committed much, of him they will ask the more" (KJV).

The main point of this Scripture is to emphasize the fact that we are all held accountable for our knowledge, resources gift, and abilities; that God has given us. He has blessed us with so much greatness, and if we are given much, then He expects that much more from us. We must keep in mind that these blessings come from the Lord, and He realizes that humans are not perfect. We can't do anything right without His help and His Holy Spirit dwelling within us. God knows that we all have weaknesses and that without Him we are nothing. John 15:5 puts it best, "I am the vine; you are the branches. If you remain in me and I in you, you will bear much fruit; apart from me you can do nothing." But we "can do all things through Christ that strengthens" us (Philippians 4:13).

Many times, we are so broken by things and people that have betrayed us that our brokenness casts a spirit of fear, discouragement, doubt, depression, and loneliness. We reside in a dark place that hides us away from our fears and tragedies. Betrayal strips us of our true identity, making us think that we are victims instead of victors.

The sad thing is that most betrayal comes when you least expect it. It always happens from your inside circle—family, friends, people to whom you've devoted your life. The ones who should be protecting you, watching over you, and keeping you out of harm's way. Instead, they become the very harm that you hide from, your worst nightmare and most tragic testimony.

Every day, we must fight our way back to the person we really are, but the wall of humiliation has been

built so high that it becomes difficult for the victim to climb over. It's this wall that pulls us away from living the best life, or should I say the blessed life that God has planned for us.

The truth is we never fully know God's plan for our lives and/or why our lives take the paths they do; lonely, sad, depressing paths—the kind that lead us to question God.

I would like to introduce you to the three deadliest types of betrayal: Personal, Mental, and Physical. Each one has its place; each is assigned to you, but they all prepare you for the next level of elevation in life. God sends us through a season in life that leads us from preparation to completion. Today, when we look at the world, we notice that darkness has crept into our schools, homes, jobs, relationships, and even media (television, radio, and internet).

Oftentimes, when pressure, sorrow, or trouble hit, we fear that it will never end. We throw in the towel; we head down Give Up Ave and turn left on No Longer Standing on God's Promise Boulevard. When this occurs, not only must we hold fast and trust God in every situation, but also take comfort that "every situation is not designed to take us around our problems, but to lead us through them."

~ Carey Gidron Sr ~

If we trust and follow Him like Judah, although it may be difficult, he will lead us to our promise land. So many victories are lost and have gone to the grave because we fail to trust God through it all. Sin is very potent and contagious; it affects our lives in ways untold. Sin and distrust puts us in a place all by ourselves because they separate us from God, His promise and benefits. Sin requires spiritual sanitation. I'm reminded of the lyrics, "What can wash away my sins? Nothing but the blood of Jesus." No longer do we have to live in sin or distrust because Jesus paid the cost with His blood.

Although sin seems pleasurable, it's only temporal. God loved us so much that He took apart Himself and came into the world to redeem us. John 3:16 says, "For God so loved the world that He gave His only begotten Son that whosoever believe in Him shall not perish but have everlasting life." Jesus' birth, death, and resurrection saved us from death; it redeemed us from our fears and betrayals of life. God's love is everlasting. It doesn't change.

God stands between us and our fatal mistakes, our innermost betrayals. His love is there to wake us up and help us realize that He loves us. Despite our pain and disappointments in life, His love eliminates the excuse of being a victim of betrayal. It eliminates the captivity of your mindset and unlocks your door of being an overcomer and survivor. His love challenges us to trust Him and never give up. Every person who has ever experienced betrayal, if they are not careful, can find themselves imprisoned by it—physically, mentally, and spiritually.

I have experienced them all, but none was as life threatening as self-betrayal. I almost died; I lost my mind, my trust and confidence in life. I began to need man's approval to have self-worth. My value in life was destroyed to the point that I found myself gravitating to every man I met in ministry calling them father because I felt the need for protection and approval. It became so bad that I found myself in a grown man's body doing grown-man things like getting married and starting a family, but never maturing the little boy who was still locked on the inside.

This little boy was damaged beyond repair. **"I found myself in the work field hire as a man, but in private producing like a boy"** ~ Carey Gidron, Sr.~ I walked away from job after job, because I was getting deeper into my brokenness and I just could not focus. I allowed my betrayal to influence my life and I soon became unstable—never capable of standing on my own as a man because the boy on the inside was still crushed and destroyed. I was unable to have healthy relationships because I was still a little boy on the inside who never recovered from being destroyed.

My mind was in a daily battle. I began to act out in ways that were beyond my parent's control. I became untamed and undisciplined to the point that my mom and dad were faced with making the very difficult decision to put me in a children's mental institution. Charter Barkley was a North Side psychiatric hospital. I was put in a room with kids who wore straitjackets, and sometimes I was locked in a room by myself, away from my family and friends. I only received a phone call once a week. I recall having to sleep in the hallway a few times, so I could be monitored. I was given 30 to 40 milligrams of a medication called *Ritalin* (*methylphenidate*), which is used to treat attention deficit disorder (ADD).

My parents refused to give up on me because they loved me so much. One day while at Charter Barkley, I remember going to the bathroom and hearing a voice say, "Carey, I have use of you." Now, I must confess that I thought it was the medication; but in retrospect, I now know it was the voice of God. My parents spent thousands of dollars on my treatment trying to save me, not knowing that my issues were bigger than what appeared; In fact, my issue lived in our home. It grew up with me and was supposed to protect me instead of destroying me; can you say "Betrayal"? I felt lost and confused in the worst way. I knew that I didn't need medication or to be institutionalized; I needed to be rescued. But how could I tell my parents? How?!!

You see, life throws curve balls in every direction, and if you are not careful you will get hit every time, with the worst curve balls in life, and that's when it's up to you to decide if you would become a victim of circumstance and situations, or a winner. I've discovered in my brokenness that "**just because you're broken doesn't mean you are destroyed**" ~Carey Gidron Sr.~

You have to fight in this thing called life, fight and push through and toward God's plan for your life. Every battle and disappointment in life is not to destroy you, but to make you bigger, better, and greater to let you know who's on your side, and whose side you are on. **"I have discovered that in life we all must experience a battle that sometimes outweighs our strength but not our God!!"** ~Carey Gidron Sr. ~

Please keep in mind that every battle is defeated by a principle, and every principle is attached to some kind of battle in life

~ Carey Gidron, Sr.

CHAPTER 3

Injured on Duty

The Experience

It was June 19, 2014, a Thursday night. This day began very differently for me. My life had been a complete wreck all week, month, and year. Nothing seemed to make life better for me. I had experienced disappointment after disappointment, and no peace, joy, life, or God could be found! I had been out of a job for the past year and now things had really turned for the worse for me and my family. I couldn't afford rent, the church membership had gone down, our water had been turned off, and I was ready to end it all.

But before I did that, I thought I would give it one more try, one more push, one more pursuit of happiness, and so I woke up and prayed to the God in whom I have trusted at that time for more than 28 years of my life. I asked Him if He would please take over this day and just give me another chance to live again.

The day before, I had taken a test at school and I scored extremely low. I don't know exactly what happened, but I knew it could not be correct, and so on the next day I was scheduled to retest, but I did it differently this time. I prayed over the test, and in my mind I said to

God that if he loved me, please give me peace of mind and allow me to refocus so I could do better than before!

After praying over the test, I then proceeded to take it. And it was as if someone had marked every answer for me—the answers began to just jump up off the pages, my understanding of the questions was so much more clear, and yes, I passed the test, scoring very high.

I was so excited; I begin to give God praise like in the days of old when I first met the Lord. I went home and rested, but before I took my usual nap, I prayed again. Later on, my wife and children returned home, and I talked to them for a while when something said listen to your voice mail. So I did, and to my surprise I had a message from a company I had applied to telling me that I got the job. I praised the Lord even more. Later that evening, I prepared myself to go and support one of the local pastors in his installation service.

As I prepared to go there, the enemy came into my home like a whirlwind and pushed me twenty steps back into a place that I felt like I was coming out of. Me and my wife began to have a big argument over some stupid stuff, and I stormed out of the house so angry I was hoping and praying that this will all end, praying that I could just die and never return again.

When I finally reached my destination at the church, the service was going strong… man, I was so empty inside, empty to the point I could not talk to anyone for the first time in my life. I felt like I was a total stranger in the church, a place I knew all too well and now I'm a stranger—WOW!!! The music didn't move me; the words of encouragement didn't move me. I mean for the first time in my life, I truly was going through the motions of church. The preacher preached the Word as if he knew exactly what I was going through, but yet I was not moved. People were shouting and dancing but I felt nothing. In fact, if I'd had a gun, I would have killed myself right then and there.

After the preacher was done, I left and got into my car. I didn't know how I was going to get back home. All I had was three bucks and some change and the gas tank was completely on "E." However, I got into my car and drove up the street and looked at the church where I served as pastor, wondering and thinking that I can't do this anymore, and then I did a U turn and drove to the gas station on 83rd and Halsted Street to get some gas. I went into the store and I put two dollars on pump 3. I began to use the little change that I had to buy some candy, but I didn't have enough, so I put the change back in my pocket, and I left the store to pump my gas.

And that's when it happened! A man who I had never met before in my life came up to me; he asked if I had some change. As he waited, he said I was a preacher. Now normally I don't stand outside and talk to people. If you would have seen this brother, you probably wouldn't have stopped to talk to him either; he was smelly, balmy-looking, clothes were dirty and his skin was dirty I was saying in my mind, God, please let me get inside of my car safely, the truth is the God in me would not allow me to reject him because of his appearance.

As the man began to speak, he never asked for change a second time, but he began to speak great change into my life. This brother grabbed me by my hand and said, "You, sir, are a true man of God, and God has great plans for you." He said the time has come. He said I don't know you, and he didn't, so I thought in my mind what Mom used to tell us all the time, **"Think it not strange when a stranger shall come to you, because it may be an angel unaware."** He said God wants all of you, God said why have you turned your heart away from Him. God has found great faith in you, and that I must not turn away from God now. He said God has a plan that shall come fast for you in this season.

He began to tell me that I have been through a lot this year, but don't give up. He said that God must test you at this level, so that when He takes you to the next level, He can trust you to handle all that comes with it. He said your name is so great in the heavens, God is requiring all of you. He wants every part of you. The man said that God asked why are you not praying anymore? He said don't worry about the cars, houses, and money. Don't depend on the people or the church. Seek God. He said, "Sir, I'm begging you—seek God!!! God has so much for you He just wants you to himself…"

What really got me is that he said he had not come to rebuke me but to heal me and restore me; and when he said that, something in my spirit said look into his eyes now. Mind you, it was night outside, and when I looked into his eyes it was as if his eyes didn't exist. They were so light, the glassiest light, bright gray eyes I have ever seen in my life. The more I tried to look into his eyes, the more I couldn't; my eyes began to burn and water up all at the same time. I knew then that the Holy Spirit had taken on the form of a human just to speak to me. He said that my ministry is worldwide, is bigger than what I could ever imagine. He said Africa, Japan, and many other countries are waiting on me. He began to call out many names of the great preachers of today, and he said my name was greater than these. After he spoke to me, he grabbed me and held me and began to pray. Man, this might sound crazy, but for the first time since I was a child, I felt like I was in the arms of my father, and a great peace came over me, and he took my right hand and held it for what seemed like a long time, but it was just for a few seconds, and the entire right side of my body began to explode with a great shaking and tingling. Man, I had never had this experience before in my life, but the greatest peace came over me on this night, amen!

I was so injured on duty and somehow this man knew it. He changed my life. Unexpectedly, my strength came back; like Samson, my hair was now growing again, Samson who had become enslaved by his desires. Like David, he defeated a lion but couldn't strangle his lust. He destroyed the captivity of chains and ropes but was bound by his hunger. He charred the enemy's harvests yet was enflamed with lust for their women. He was strong, courageous, but not really in control. The champion was captured by the enemy and conquered by desires of the flesh!

Samson is on duty and working in the spirit of scandalous ways. When reading his story, you can't but wonder if Samson felt any sense of shame playing with the enemy? Samson now became an embarrassment to Israel. When those in great leadership fall to temptation, the church becomes their worst enemy for some reason, as if those in the church had never made any mistakes. Now please don't get me wrong. I think that every leader should be held accountable for their actions. The Bible puts it like this (Luke 12:48): "But he that knew not, and did commit things worthy of stripes, shall be beaten with few stripes. For unto whomsoever much is given, of him shall be much required: and to whom men have committed much, of him they will ask the more." The seeds that Samson is sowing in Gaza lead to the path of his destruction with Delilah. Sin has consequences. Romans 6:23 (KJV) says: "**For the wages of sin is death**; but the gift of God is eternal life through Jesus Christ our Lord."

People are fully aware of Samson's presence; he wasn't trying to keep a low profile. The Philistines set up the trap against Samson by securing the city gates; they thought to themselves that they had him, he was locked in; but little they know. He was in full strength and he was on duty. The Bible says that Samson ripped the gates off the hinges with his enormous might and carried them to Hebron, 40 miles away! Say what?!! This guy was strong and he was no joke!

According my studies, it's estimated that these gates may have weighed over a thousand pounds. In Biblical times the gates of cities were considered the symbol of their strength. By removing the city gate, Samson caused Gaza great embarrassment. You may look at this story and say it is unreal, but I must say that when you are on an assignment and have the favor of God upon your life, anything is possible, even moving gates. The Bible says it like this in Matthew 17:20: "And Jesus said unto them, Because of your unbelief: for verily I say unto you, If ye have faith as a grain of mustard seed, ye shall say unto this mountain, Remove hence to yonder place; and it shall remove; and nothing shall be impossible unto you." Samson's faith and his birthright, and God's promise to his mother, put him into a class by himself. There are no limits to God's power.

After the Gaza catastrophe, Samson was on the Philistine's "Most Wanted" list! Something had to be done about him, but the Philistines were too afraid to act against him by themselves. Now don't get me wrong, they wanted him and they wanted him bad! But what they wanted more than anything was the source of Samson's strength. You see, when the devil knows that you are damaged goods and that you have been injured on duty and you are still standing, your strength stops the enemy in his tracks and you leave him confused, trying to figure out how do you have the strength to go on. To the enemy, you now appear to be weak because you have made great mistakes, as Samson did not look like a remarkably strong person. That's why the Bible says in Zechariah 4:6, "Not by might, nor by power, but by my spirit, saith the LORD of hosts."

So now the devil is after your strength, and he sees Samson open interaction with Philistine women—and it becomes clear to the enemy what Samson's weakness is. So now the trap was set. Delilah became their "secret agent." Her name has become synonymous with seduction, and she's often blamed for Samson's fall, yet she was merely doing her job as a loyal Philistine. She turned on the charm, and Samson was very vulnerable.

Delilah pleaded with Samson to reveal the secret of his strength. What's wrong here? It should've been obvious that God was the Source of Samson's strength! The Philistines figured Samson was using trickery. Samson's lifestyle of a whoremonger was clearly misrepresenting the life of a man of God. There should be some sign; my grandfather used to say that if you got that old-time religion, then you ought to show some sign that you are chosen to serve God, it should never be private! The Bible says in Matthew 5:14: "Ye are the light of the world. A city that is set on a hill cannot be hid." The Philistines justifiably assumed that God wasn't the head of Samson's life. But how did he get so strong?

Samson thought Delilah was teasing with him, and so he teased her back, misleading her with lie after lie. Samson played the game of truth or dare; he played Russian roulette, and at the end, guess; who got the bullet? She ripped through him so smoothly and convinced him to reveal his secret. In Judges Chapter 14, Delilah bribed Samson to disclose the sacred mystery of his strength. Samson was in love with Delilah. He wasn't in his right mind. **"Rather than putting an end to this love affair with Delilah, he allowed it to put an end to him."** ~Prophet Carey Gidron~

Frustrated Delilah sobbed and questioned his love, and so he told her of his vow. I don't think he knew what love was. Samson couldn't resist his attraction for Delilah and her gift of persuasion, so he gave that which was divine to the hand of the enemy. Samson lost more than his hair; he lost the presence and Glory of God.

Yet he did not know that the Lord had departed from him. Samson was officially considered as mark down damaged goods. Samson had been known for his great disregard of the Nazarite vow, yet hadn't been punished. The truth is that he hadn't been much of a "practicing" Nazarite anyway. Samson's hair by itself didn't make him strong, but it was the commitment of his vow that produced his strength; this set him apart as a Nazarite. Cutting his hair; cut off his ties to God. Samson had grown bound by his appetite, blinded by his desires…and the lust of his flesh. It's no question that Samson was the strongest man of all time, and accomplished a level of strength that not even a good workout at the gym could produce but only a God—our God.

But don't just think of Samson's strength, because so many of us have more in common with him than we think: man or woman, young or old, strong or weak. We keep making the same bad decisions, day after day, year after year. We're either oblivious to them or we're indifferent, or we feel powerless to change, and we allow the enemy to come and rob us on a daily basis of our promises from God. We constantly make promises and vows to God, and for some reason God keeps His end of the deal, but we break our vow over and over again, and God is so faithful, He restores us in spite of our mess-ups. Hosea 6:1-3 (New NIV) says: "Come, let us return to the Lord. He has torn us to pieces but He will heal us; He has injured us but He will bind up our wounds. After two days He will revive us; on the third day He will restore us that we may live in His presence. Let us acknowledge the Lord; let us press on to acknowledge Him. As surely as the sun rises, He will appear; He will come to us like the winter rains, like the spring rains that water the earth."

Amen.

CHAPTER 4

THE WRONG ATTACHMENTS

(I'm Just like You)
Mental Betrayal

I have experienced overwhelming mental betrayal in my life. Recently, God blessed me with the vision to take the ministry to the next level. He confirmed to me that He would bless the ministry if I would only trust and believe in Him. I must tell you that I'd previously done that with everything that was inside of me, and God proved Himself to be faithful. This year marks 28 years of my life that I have dedicated unto the Lord, ministry, and God's people. I have done my best to live a clean and righteous life.

Although I've made some mistakes, as I am human, I have somehow managed to still stay on course and trust God. I've endured being lied on by people I don't even know—those who I've never even met… many of whom were in the church. The religious community has filled me with so many fears and disappointments in my lifetime.

I remember one of my first experiences as a pastor. The church was doing well, and one week I took the ministry to an out-of-town conference in Sardis MS. I trusted one of the evangelists who I truly believed had my back to preach in my place; little did I know that she had other plans. She began to yield to a spirit of pride and tried to overtake the ministry for her benefit. This was one of my first encounters with a member who I trusted who came up against me in a way that I could not imagine. I was reminded of Proverbs 11:2, which states, "When pride comes, then comes; disgrace, but with humility comes wisdom."

For some reason, after that occurrence, a great spirit of unfaithfulness, lack of commitment, disobedience, and rebellion followed. It was so bad that I worried myself sick, and I mean to the point that it led to me nearly having a heart attack and a mild stroke at the age of 36; my blood pressure went up so high and I've been on medication ever since. I was so stressed about this ministry that I'd devoted my life to, that I had neglected my wife and children for what I called doing the work of the ministry, My family has known life without electricity as well as sleeping in a car. We've had to live with my in-laws—all for what I call the church and the people of God. My life had been shattered because of church hurt- the true silent killer within the church…

I have been rejected by pastors and bishops, those for whom I had the utmost respect. They used me because of the prophetic gift God gave me. As long as my gift benefited them, as long as I raised money for their offerings, they were fine with me. But the moment my gift matured and no longer served their personal agendas, I was no longer welcomed to preach in their churches. Preachers have smiled in my face and talked about me behind my back. I've been called an opportunist. I've had people try to destroy my marriage by gossiping and spreading rumors. Church hurt has been the greatest hurt I have ever experienced.

Oftentimes when pressure, sorrow, or trouble strikes, we fear that it will never end. But, like David in the Bible, I would encouraged myself not to throw in the towel or give up. I'd reminded myself to stand on the promises of God and to hold fast and trust Him to be God.

Although I knew the word of God, it was not always easy to apply, there were times where I had no idea what I was doing in my life, much less in my ministry. I had no vision for my family, which believed in me when I didn't know what was coming next. For many years, they continual to followed me, many times to a dead end. I know my wife and children had to be tired and ready to give up on me, but they never did. I used to blame myself, which led to self-hatred. All I could think about was how many times I'd asked them to believe in me as I believed in God; however, where God never fails, I continuously failed.

For more than 28 years, I held fast to the Gospel. I believed that if I stood on God's word, that His word would provide for me. I guess I was only fooling myself, because at some point I was preaching with no life in me…I was truly dead on the inside! I'd bought all the hype about the church and being a preacher, believing when they said that my gift would make room for me. But of everything "they" said, I never remember hearing anyone share the other side with me—the fact that the only way your gift makes room for you is if you fit what I call the "Pulpit Requirements":

1. You must be connected to someone who is well-known in the ministerial community.

2. If you have money, connections will automatically come your way.

3. The bishop must recommend you.

4. If you have a large congregation, you will be well-received.

5. If you come from a well-known family, you will be accepted.

Since none of the "Pulpit Requirements" applied to me, I was on my own to figure out how to structure myself in ministry. My father was a preacher in a small storefront Baptist church. He was not known throughout the city, which meant that I had to foster my own relationships; most, if not all of the local preachers in my inexperience season that I'd met had either lied to me or made broken promises. I can't even begin to tell you how many lies I've had to deal with in ministry—

For example, preachers, pastors, and bishops telling me to feel free to call them if I needed anything but giving me fake phone numbers. How many times I was invited to speak, only to show up to encounter different excuses—for example, I forgot you were coming, or I thought we scheduled it for next week. Like really! Never mind my disappointment, but I had to face my wife and children and explain to them what transpired. In some cases, I spent our rent money to travel to get to the promised engagement, and now there was no way to be reimbursed.

I found myself feeling worthless; I'd been seeking man's approval and validation, but now it was time to take a break because I realized just how wounded I was. I became more and more contaminated while leading God's people. I could barely lead myself, or my family. How could I be responsible to lead anyone else?

> **Con.tam.i.nate.** *Verb. Past tense: contaminated; past participle: contaminated. Meaning: to make (something) impure by exposure to or addition of a poisonous or polluting substance.*

There is such a great danger when it comes to spiritual contamination. It's not like being filled with wrongdoing, but with someone doing you wrong you become filled with anger, frustration, and bitterness. And these things can become a great sickness to the life of the believer, especially when you have an anointing upon your life that cannot be denied; you go through so many changes when you have been contaminated by the wrong spiritual leadership.

I'll never forget my experience with the wrong leadership. I remember it as clear as day. This was one of the most dangerous and fatal mistakes I have ever made in my ministry career. I was young still in ministry, I had just begun to get over my mom's death, and there was this apostle I had known since I was a teenager from the West Side of Chicago. I truly had a great deal of respect for this lady. She asked me if I would move my family to Sardis, Mississippi to pastor her church there. She promised that we would not have to worry about anything; she would provide housing, moving expenses, plus a weekly pastoral salary of $600. She did require me to give up my local church; in fact, I would preach there for two or three weeks and then fly back home to Chicago and preach at my local church. So I put one of my God-Mom Dr. Vessel in as my assistant pastor to work with my local church in Chicago.

It started out going well. We were building the ministry. Great awareness was building. We had a radio program. People's lives were truly being changed. We had just come out of a mighty revival with my spiritual mother, the late Apostle Christine Morris. She visited us there, and I'll never forget her words. She said to me, son, this is not the Lord's will. You need to come back home quickly and complete what God has given you.

I thank God for my true spiritual mother.

Right after this conversation, when mother was on the plane headed back home, the Lord gave me a dynamic message. We produced flyers and put them out all over the area, and we were even feeding the local community with fresh, hot meals. The ministry was growing and it was doing well. Sunday had come around and it was time to give this dynamic message that I had prepared. Cars were lined up alongside the road, and the parking lot was full. Finally I pulled up to the church and walked in and I was greeted by the apostle and her crew. She held me in the office giving me a great rebuke because I had changed the sound system to make it conducive to what we were trying to produce in the service. She held me so long that one of her people got up and preached to the large crowd and the service. Then she told me that I could not preach for the next two weeks. I did not understand what was going on. How had the enemy crept into the heart of the apostle and her team?

From that time on, it was just confusion after confusion, even to the point that late one night she and her team came to the home that was being provided for me and my family. They burst in the home and began yelling and screaming, awakening my children. It was her and about four other people, one of whom was a police officer who had her gone with her as if I was to be threatened. The apostle and her team were so disrespectful to my wife and I until I made the statement, "Please leave my home." She then replied, "This is not your home, this is my home." To make a long story short, right after that confusion me and my wife and children decided take a trip back home to Chicago to be with my family. While at home in Chicago, we received one of the most devastating calls ever from the apostle and her team, telling us that we could not return back to what we considered our home. After giving up a job in Chicago that was making good money, and leaving my ministry, which was growing and prospering, and leaving our families in Chicago, we were told that what we considered as home in Mississippi was not our home and that we could not return. They took our belongings both personal and private, put them in garbage bags, threw them onto a moving truck, and sent them back to Chicago.

It was devastating for me, but it was even more devastating for my wife…I kind of felt like Joseph because I consider her as family.… Do you remember the story of Joseph and his brothers? As I look deep into Joseph's life and see how his life really relates to mine and yours of today, there are many situations in life of great bitterness, hatred, and betrayal that we all can attest to experiencing in some way or other, whether by friends or outsiders such as co-workers, classmates, next-door neighbors, and so on. Unfortunately for Joseph, his experience with betrayal started at home. This was unlike mine, which happened inside of the church. **WOW.**

"Family is the core of your existence, the reason why we all live."

~ Carey Gidron, Sr.~

Joseph was hated and sold into slavery by his brothers, all because he shared his dreams too soon with those he trusted to celebrate him and not just tolerate him. His base of betrayal starts in Genesis 37:5. But even before that there were problems.

Joseph's betrayal started with his family before he was born; his secret betrayal steamed long before it reached his life experience. Rachel and Leah both tried to outdo each other in producing babies. Not only that, but they involved outsiders—their hand maidens Zilpah and Bilhah—in an effort to betray each other and get one man's interest. This family betrayal was generational. The battle of betrayal was so omnipresent between the two sisters until a curse of betrayal had passed on to Joseph and his brothers. This was truly a seed sown and a seed grown between them,

His father slept with his father's concubine Bilhah, and Jacob got word of this betrayal. This action by him was considered as a great betrayal because it caused Ruben not only to lose his father's favor but also his inheritance.

Jacob exercised his absolute authority and appointed Joseph as his inheritor. It was just right for Jacob to make such a decision. Jacob felt the need to have someone he could trust. I often wonder if Joseph felt, like me, "What did I do to deserve this?" Joseph now wore the coat of many colors that's mentioned in the study of the text. The correct Hebrew translation is not a coat of many colors but "a lengthy or long overcoat."

Back then, the coats were sleeveless and stopped at the knees, and they were worn by men of hard employment. This coat was long near the ankles, and was what we call today a trench coat, and it was worn by those who did not have to work.

When Joseph appeared before his brothers with his new coat of favor and blessings that his father had awarded him, there was trouble in the camp because that coat signified to them Joseph's superiority over them. Now that became a problem for his older brothers, although Ruben lost that right of being the rightful beneficiary because of his deceitfulness in sleeping with his stepmother.

"I have discovered on this journey of life that the enemy doesn't just attack you because of who you are! He attacks you because you remind him of God, you remind him of the authority that God has given you over his every plan, and you remind him of the position he used to have and could have had."

~ Carey Gidron, Sr.

Jacobs's decision to favor Joseph over his brothers came with a great price, and if truth be told it really had nothing to do with Ruben's mistake as much as it had to do with his choice of love for Josephs' mother. The beginning of Verse 3 in Genesis 37 gives us the real root of the bitterness against Joseph. "Now Israel loved Joseph more than all his children, because he was the son of his old age." Favor is not fair, and it developed great dysfunction and conflict between the brothers. They hated him even more for his dreams and for his favor. This of course led to their betrayal of Joseph, which sent him eventually to Egypt. I can only imagine the hurt, pain, and disbelief that Joseph was experiencing. It's one thing if your haters are on the outside, but another when they are on the inside! Your family, friends, the people who you trust with your very life, the ones who you expect to love you no matter what. I must say that this is something, but God always has a plan for us. In fact, He says in Deuteronomy 31:6 (NIV): "Be strong and courageous. Do not be afraid or terrified because of them, for the Lord your God goes with you; he will never leave you nor forsake you."

Joseph's betrayal had nothing to do with him but started from a generational curse, like what I had to experience, when I was a child. You see, generational curses are so real, and if they are not put to an end, they will all continue from generation to generation. But today I become a game changer—the curse stops here!

I believe that the Lord uses trials, difficulty, and pain to equip us for more effective service to Him. Look at Joseph's track record during his time and season of betrayal. He was sold into slavery to the Egyptians. As an Egyptian captive, Joseph exceeded all expectations in running Potiphar's household. Even though Potiphar's wife accused Joseph of molesting her, and he was sentenced to prison. While in jail, God still anointed his gift to interpret a dream and predicted that Pharaoh's butler would be restored to his former position. Fortunately, once he was employed again, and Pharaoh had a mysterious dream, this same butler remembered the young Hebrew's amazing gift.

I learn two things from this example: (1) never look for everyone in your enter circle to be by you 100% of the time; and (2) even if it's family betrayal, which is always at the back door, as we see in the life of Joseph, God will never allow you to be forgotten. His word says "I have been young, and *now* am old; yet have I not seen the righteous forsaken, nor his seed begging bread" (Ps 37:25).

CHAPTER 5

THE DEATH EFFECTS

(My Silent Tears)

Often, I wonder how I still have my right mind with all of the things that I've had to endure in my life. On a cold, cold morning in November I was in a deep sleep dreaming about a funeral. There were a lot of people gathered—family, friends, a lot of faces that I was extremely familiar with—I can remember it like it was literally a few hours ago. This moment in my life plays over and over in my mind. It always takes me into an extremely deep, dark place, because I believe that it's when I first discovered that the call of seer and Prophet was upon my life. I was at this funeral and the preacher had just completed his sermon. It was time for the final view. I got in the line, and as I was walking up there were a lot of people standing over the casket. I could only see the color of the casket. I'll never forget the color—it was this gray silver-like metal color and it was just about my time to walk around and see who was in the casket. Instantly, as soon as I begin to peek over into the casket to see who it was, I awakened. I woke up, saying I have to get back to the funeral; I have to get back to the funeral. My cousin's brother said to me, "Carey, wake up. Wake up."

I said, "Yeah, what's wrong?"

"We cannot find lil' Jessie," he said. "Have you seen him?"

I said, "No, but I'll go with you guys and help you find him."

I'll never forget this day. I got dressed, got in the vehicle with my mom, and we drove back to the area where there was supposed to have been a shooting reported, driving near the mouth of an alleyway when I said "Stop!!!" to my mom.

"What's wrong?" she asked.

I said I needed to get out, I had to find lil' Jessie.

So she stopped the vehicle, and his brothers and I then began to walk. I walked ahead of them and I could constantly hear something in my right ear. I remember my ear burning like fire. I could hear something say keep walking forward, and then it said to make a left in this gangway. I was familiar with the gangway because the people who lived in the house nearby were friends of ours. As I walked down the gangway I heard something say, now, look over in the vacant lot next to the gangway. There was something like a deep ditch in this vacant lot, and when I looked over in the ditch I saw my cousin's lifeless body. As I write I cannot stop the tears from flowing as I see this so clearly.

I jumped over the gate and instantly grabbed his body and turned him over because he was faced down; I discover that he had been shot in the face I was terrified scared beyond life so I instantly let him go. I begin to run down the street screaming and hollering, hollering and screaming; his brothers and I, we all saw this. My cousin's death has left an unforgettable stain in my life and memory but I'm still standing....

When I was 16, my grandfather died in my arms while I was giving him a bath. Then, my cousin's brother was killed by gang members. Lil' James was the brother of Lil Jessie the cousin I'd found dead when

I was 14 years old. I'd begun my first work in ministry by this time, at the age of 22, but after that news, I had to close it down because his death hit me so hard. I finally got myself back together and restarted the work of ministry.

Then in 2005, my mom died. Her death was so devastating, so quick, and I was so unprepared. Mom passed away without a moment's notice. We did everything together. She was a pillar of my life—a true strong tower. I battled in my mind how I was going to move forward without her. I found myself preaching to God's people empty and lost in the heart. One day, God spoke to me and said it was time to let go and move on, and so I did…until about a year and a half later, in January of 2008, when my father died.

For years, my dad and I could not see eye to eye on anything. Many times, I thought I knew as much as he did, but the fact of the matter was that dad always knew best. This man would do anything to protect and love us. He watched over his family and gave all he had, even if it was the shoes off his own feet or the clothes off his back. My dad used to think that I wanted to preach like other big-named preachers; the truth is that I just wanted to be like my dad. Right after mom died, I think she must've had a conversation with God and asked Him to improve the relationship between me and my dad because it wasn't until after she died that we got close. We talked every day; I checked on him or he would call me. We became so close—I was the spitting image of him.

On Sunday, January 6, 2008, he came to my church. I preached a message entitled, "God's Combination to Man's Heart." Dad was so excited and touched by that sermon. After service that day, he told me that he was considering joining my church. However, God called him home that Thursday night. I lost it. I questioned God—asked Him why He hated me? I wanted to know why He would allow my father and me to become so close just to take him away from me. My dad and I had just gotten to the place where nothing mattered other than the fact that we were father and son. I hated myself because I never expected my dad to die so quickly, like my mom did. I really thought that we would have more time together, time to start all over and correct the many things that I'd done wrong in my life as it pertained to my dad.

I remember being so angry with God. Here I was serving the Lord with all of my heart, and I discovered every time I begin to make some form of elevation or new start in my life, those who were close to me were always snatched away, leaving me behind stripped, in despair, angry, depressed, frustrated, lonely, and sad. For what it's worth, I thought I would pass this incredible testimony on to you, the reader, and yet let you know that when death comes, it is like a thief in the night. It leaves you empty with so many questions like: God, why did this have to happen? Why couldn't you leave them and take me? Why did you have to take them at such an early age? These are the questions that run through your mind day in and day out, not once or twice but as a constant thing that plays in your mind and in your heart because you've been so attached to those loved ones all of your life.

In most cases, I can tell you my anger lasted for a long time. I was angry with God. I mean I really wrestled. I had a hard time getting over the deaths of my cousins, my grandfather, my mother, and my father. I could not understand or get a direct answer from God as to why He allowed all of them to pass at the time of me doing something great, but at such a young age I felt robbed of my joy! Of my peace! Of my sanity!

After wrestling with God for quite some time, finally the Lord gave me a direct word from the bowels of the Holy Spirit that immediately set me free from mental captivity and emotional bondage. Please allow me to share that word with you today. It was life-changing to me.

I was riding in my car one day and the Holy Spirit spoke to me: "**Your family is no longer in the past. They are now in your future.**"

Take time and think about these words. It blew my mind as soon as I heard these words. I knew God was trying to let me know immediately that it was my time to finally be free from my mental and spiritual torment. Even though after this word I still felt like I was going through something, but I heard those words again: Your family is no longer in the past. They are now in your future.

Wow. In other words, look forward to seeing them again, look forward to reuniting. Smiling, hugging, and celebrating a new reunion in Heaven, for Heaven is your goal. I could have shouted all over that highway at something so simple and so clear, that one day you will see them again as you reach your goal to make it into Heaven.

I believe in that moment that God was trying to tell me to change how I looked at things and see differently; instead of seeing our families as being dead or in the past, start seeing them fully alive in Heaven and understand that you will one day truly be reunited. Our time on this earth is not even a blink of an eye compared to the eternal time frame that is waiting for us in Heaven. I have discovered that you have to step back and look at the big picture. We are all going to die and make our crossover into judgment, with no exceptions, no matter who you are or where you are. As long as Jesus delays his coming, you will one day have to die; some just go sooner than others.

When you die is not relevant, but what you do with the time that you have down here on the earth is what really matters…life is quality and not quantity, when you really grasp the meaning of the words that the Holy Spirit spoke to me, you understand that you should actually do it the way the Bible says in Philippians 4:4: "**Rejoice** in the LORD always." **I** will **say** it again: **Rejoice** and believe God, and don't throw in the towel. Proverbs 3:5 says "Trust in the LORD with all your heart; and **lean** not to your own understanding." Know that God has a plan for your life; His plan doesn't change, His will doesn't change, and everyone will fulfill every ounce of God's will before leaving this earth.

I want to tell someone like me, when you experience the loss of your loved one, and maybe you've set in the valley of no more hope and decided that you were going to quit or wallow in the past and eventually die miserably sad, frustrated, and angry—I want to tell you that's not how it has to end. I am a living testimony that even with your loss there is truly great gain. Too many people are bound up with things that have happened to them in their past. They cannot let go of some of the bad things that may have occurred in their past, and as a result their past slowly starts to eat away and tear into them, snatching every part of their existence away from them. Then you find yourself slipping into depression, loss of weight, the spirit of oppression, not wanting to live anymore, having no more dreams and hopes and desires—all because you allowed yourself to slide down the slippery slope of bondage and become locked into what used to be versus what God has in mind for you.

I know the effects of death; it causes you to completely shut down due to pain and heartache; it corrupts your ability to look forward to anything new. But I am so glad that you're taking time to read this book, because today your life is about to change in spite of who has passed away: You have to continue to hold on to God's Promise. Today I speak these words of life to you: Let it go. It's time to move on. Scripture says in Luke 9:62: "But Jesus said to them, No one having put his hand to the plow and looking back is fit for the kingdom of God." And Philippians 3:13-14 says: "**One thing** I do: **Forgetting** what is **behind** and reaching toward what is ahead, I press on toward the goal to win the prize for which God has called me in Christ Jesus."

Please take time to listen to these words. There's so much life in these verses. Forgetting those things that are behind, and reaching toward greater things, perfectly lines up with the revelation that the Holy Spirit shared with me to let the death of my loved ones go and to look forward and to press forward toward the goal of one day seeing them again. First Corinthian's 9:10 says: "He who plows should plow in hope and he who threshes in hope should be a partaker of hope." These verses teach us so strongly that we should forever continue to plow toward God with whatever ounce of time that we have left here on earth, and not only should we continue to move forward and plow toward our hopes and our dreams and our hearts' desires and in our minds, but we should also be participate in those dreams. Work your vision while you're still on earth, and really believe that when you die, you will be completed, you will have finished your journey and completed your task here and that day will come when you will reunite with all of your loved ones who have passed on to be with the Lord before your time. Heaven is going to be the final and ultimate reward for the life of every believer, which includes you.

The Bible tells us that we cannot even begin to think or imagine all of the good things that God will have in store for the life of those who trust Him and believe Him and make their way into glory. One thing we do know for sure is that we will all be given the two greatest rewards that any believer can ever hope to receive once we cross over into Heaven: We will forever be united with God and his son Jesus Christ, able to have direct contact and fellowship with both of them for the rest of eternity; and here's what I love about it—the day will come that we will be able to reunite with all of our loved ones who died in Christ.

Holding onto this revelation and this truth bought so much life to me that it gave me a jumpstart and put me back on track. It pushed me ahead and put the demand on me to live again. It put a demand on me to survive. I have to be honest with you: As difficult and as hard as it was, I am yet able to stand and say that I am a survivor from every death effect. Yes, trust you me there are going to be days when you feel so blindsided by the storms that you have experienced in life that regardless of how much you prayed and how much you fasted how much memorization of Scripture you've done, pleading and begging and ranting and raving—there are some storms that only God and your Faith can deliver you from.

As much as I was angry with God, He didn't get upset with me. He didn't even flinch. You see, God is not moved by your anger and frustrations, He's only moved by your trust and your faith. Scripture reminds us that we must cast down everything that exalts itself against the very knowledge of God. Are you hearing what the Scripture says? Tear down!—dismantle!—everything that comes up against what you have already seen God do and you've seen God deliver. You've seen God change lives, and that's what saved me; that's what delivered me; that's what gave me my mind, my faith, my hope, my joy, and my peace all back.

Peter put it this way: "Do not be surprised at the painful trials you are suffering as though something strange were happening to you, but rejoice that you participate in the sufferings of Christ so that you may be overjoyed when his glory is revealed" (1 Peter 4:12 -13). I don't know about you, but when I am in the middle of something major, I have just learned how to trust God's word, to take comfort in His promise. God will never put on you more than you can handle; if it happens to you, it's only because you were designed to handle it. 1 Peter 5:6 says: Humble yourselves therefore under the mighty hand of God, that he may exalt you in due time: KJV

Over these last 40+ years, with the strength and peace of God to completely sustain me, I've pressed through death pain, anger, depression, and frustration and I can honestly say I pursued true intimacy with God. I've never learned more about God. I've heard God speak more clearly to me during these trying times and trials of my life. I would venture to say that nearly everything God said He would do, He has performed it and then some. I can honestly say that I'm not sure how I survived. Despite my anger and frustration, I believed that God had a plan for my life. As it says in Jeremiah 29:11, "For I know the plans I have for you, plans to prosper you and not to harm you; plans to give you hope and a future not despair."

This experience taught me that we must live as though it's our last day, according to God's plan and purpose. Although I know and have convinced myself that God's plan for my life would come to pass, it didn't change the many bleak and overwhelming obstacles and realities that came from day to day in my life. I was a young pastor, husband, and father who had lost my job from a local bank; I was in danger of losing my home; my car was on the list to be repossessed; my marriage was on the edge of ending because I couldn't provide proper living security. Week after week, I was giving my wife broken promises, telling her that things were going to get better, while we were living on broken pieces.

Life was at its worst; I was hanging on tooth and nail to feed my wife and four amazing sons, fighting to pay our bills at home as well as those at the church. At this point I was at the crossroads of Given Up Avenue, Throw in the Towel Boulevard, and Never Look Back Road, unsure if life would ever get better! I believe the Lord uses trials, difficulties, and pain to equip us for more effective service to Him.

CHAPTER 6

MOVING FORWARD

Discovery is quite difficult, especially when it's not in your favor or in the direction that you desire. The journey of pastoring started for me in 2005, during a very strange and vulnerable season in my life. I remember it like it was yesterday...

I was just five years into my marriage and a third-time dad. I'd been invited to speak at a church that March. At that time, I was a member of a church called Monument of Faith, under the leadership of Apostle R.D. Henton. I went to preach for this small church on 59th Street in Chicago, unaware of the fact that this church did not have a sitting pastor. I was invited by one of the members (who was a friend of mine) after ministering the Word of God on a previous occasion.

When I preached at that church, a group of people, including some of the deacons, asked if I would mind coming back to speak again. At that time, they informed me that they were without a pastor. Once I cleared it with Apostle Henton, I let them know that I would indeed be able to make the return engagement.

I was totally unaware that they were looking at this as a sermon interview for pastoral selection; I just thought I was going back because they enjoyed my preaching. This is where the confusion started. The church had a minister there already who desired to become the pastor of the church. I had no clue about the any of this—I'd never even met him until I went back the second time, when I tried to greet him, he treated me so coldly, and I didn't understand the reason.

I asked my friend what he thought the problem could be, and that's when he explained. The minister had gotten word that the congregation wanted me to be their pastor—I didn't even know! So, he was mad about something that I wasn't even aware of. I told my friend that I wasn't interested in the position, and that I was content being an evangelist. However, as I was leaving the church, multiple members approached me, insisting that I should be the pastor, trying to convince me that I was a Godsend.

So I contacted my pastor and spoke with him about the issue. He wanted to meet with me personally to discuss it further. We talked about a lot of things including his many ministerial experiences. At the end of our conversation he said something to me that has stayed with me even to this day. That night Apostle Henton said, "I'm not one who holds a preacher back. So, I say if God has called you to do this, always love on His people. And remember, if you discover that He didn't, never be afraid to stop and regroup…and come back home."

He taught me the greatest lesson on success when he said that success is not staying in a place that keeps you miserable just to say you did it. But true success is knowing; when your time is up and being willing to move on. This is exactly what happened to me after ten years of the many ups and downs of pastoring. I discovered how miserable I'd become all because I allowed people and their emotions to push me into a place that God had not called me to. It was not two years after becoming a pastor when those same individuals who pushed and encouraged me to become their pastor just stopped coming completely.

Some moved out of town—just up and left me. I was left with a church and a handful of people.

I possessed no true vision for being a pastor. I was always traveling and putting on evangelistic conferences; they were more successful than the local ministry. I was still doing the work of an evangelist, not realizing that the real reason why I had so many successes was because although I had the title of "Pastor," I had the heartbeat of a Prophet and Evangelist.

There are so many great preachers like myself who choose to walk in something different from what God called them to do, all because of a great moment. But you must remember that *moments* are not *seasons*, and so often we confuse the two. Galatians 6:3 says, "If a man thinks himself to be something when he is not, he only deceives himself." You see, everyone around me could clearly see that God had called me to my first work, but I was blinded by image.

I was living out an addiction to image and not my true calling. I became more concerned with the idea of what others might say and think about me if I was to walk away from it all…knowing that God had truly assigned me to something different. My addiction to image had become so bad that it affected everything and everyone in my surroundings—my wife, my children, and even my ability to properly produce in the pulpit. I was simply operating in image-mode and not following my ordained destiny. I was lost and confused, with no real answers and no true way out.

Ironically, the title of this book came to me from a message that my then 13-year-old son, CJ, ministered at a youth conference. He began to speak to some deep issues that I had inside. I was truly at a place of giving up and ending it all; I had become worn out with the cares and pressures of life and ministry. Battling with the fact that I was 30 years into ministry as an evangelist, and had over 10 years as a pastor, yet when I looked back, I couldn't help but wonder what I had accomplished? And my answer was a big NOTHING. I'd watched so many preachers who seemed like they had just "blown up" overnight, yet I was still struggling with the same handful of members Sunday after Sunday. There was no growth and no development.

My godfather, Sam Sago, used to always say, "If we always do what we've always done, we'll always be where we've always been, so I'm having what I've never had because I'm doing what I've never done!" That was such a profound statement and caused a great awakening for me. It reminded me of the Bible story found in Genesis 26:12-13: "Then Isaac sowed in that land, and received in the same year an hundredfold: and the Lord blessed him. And the man waxed great, and went forward, and grew until he became very great."

When looking closely at this passage, I noticed that Isaac became great because of his obedience and his relationship with God. You see, it was God who released the blessings over his life. Looking closer into the passage, it is when Isaac discovered the release from God that he decided to MOVE FORWARD, and grew until he became VERY great! Although Isaac was appreciative of what God had done, he was not satisfied with the initial blessing, which had already begun to produce greatness in him. He didn't get caught up in the notion that "a little bit will do" like many do. Instead, he had tenacity to go past and MOVE FORWARD...AND GROW...UNTIL HE BECAME GREAT!!!

In his life pursuits, he discovered that true growth comes only when one is determined to keep moving forward and operate in his or her ordained purpose. This mindset takes you from just being blessed to being great.

It's recorded in Philippians 3:13-14: "Brethren, I count not myself to have apprehended: but this one thing I do, forgetting those things which are behind, and reaching forth unto those things which are before, I press toward the mark for the prize of the high calling of God in Christ Jesus."

Paul knew that the only way to progress in this walk is by allowing God to start us over and move forward. No looking back. He reminds us of the importance of staying focused to pursue and accomplish our every goal and dream. No looking back on past failures; refuse to allow distractions to be an option.

Remember God promise to give us an expected end. So if God has promised to give us an expected end, that is to say He gives you your every expectation when reaching and accomplishing your life's goals and dreams, if you have yet to receive your expected results, you must ask, "Am I fulfilling God's perfect plan? What's my next move without making the same mistake?" It is during this time when great doubt and confusion may begin to set in your mind. However, you must step out of your now and into your tomorrow; reposition your surroundings, thoughts, goals and vision.

This is a key lesson for the believer: When you obey God, you can expect the unexpected to happen when you MOVE FORWARD! In God's plan and vision, there is only one way to move in the king-dom—MOVE FORWARD! When we move forward, the Lord will open the door! There are some things we will never accomplish except by obeying God's voice. It takes God to bring us into a place of victory; but God demands obedience from us. Obedience pushes us to a place called "Forward"!

Yes, you can expect obstacles, resistance, and hardship. Expect to let God be God in your life in order to grow. Just don't turn back, because your turning back may cause you to die. Your success depends upon your desire and ability to discover. In spite of your situation, there can NEVER be a time or place in our lives that we stop moving forward!!!

CHAPTER 7

The Price of Disobedience / Promotion

Spiritual Betrayal

We all go through that stage of disobedience to our parents, and even to God. The strange thing is that in most cases we are fully aware that there is a price to pay; yet for some odd reason, we willingly take that chance with God, not knowing what the exact price of such acts of disobedience will be.

I'm reminded of the story in the Bible about a man named Jonah. He decided to do what he wanted instead of being obedient to God. Jonah did not go to Nineveh; he went where he wanted to go. Jonah felt like he could run away from God and ignore his instructions, which proved to be a big mistake.

According to Jonah 1:3, "But Jonah arose to flee Tarshish from the presence of the Lord." He got word that in Joppa there was a ship going to Tarshish, so he paid his fare and hopped aboard thinking he'd be able to escape God. Consequently, he entered a spirit of disobedience unto God, which was accompanied by life curses as mentioned in

Deuteronomy 28:15: "But it shall come to pass, if thou wilt not hearken unto the voice of the Lord thy God, to observe to do all his commandments and his statutes which I command thee this day; that all these curses shall come upon thee and overtake thee." Jonah chose the path of disobedience unto God and had to pay the price.

Although not a good thing, I am totally able to identify with Jonah's situation, and can testify that disobeying God not only leads in direct punishment from Him, but your life's choices will also be cursed.

In reflecting upon my past and hurts, I realized that one of the major problems I encountered resulted from engaging in ministry prematurely, or during what I call "The Incubator Stage." This is when a person who is born and bred into ministry goes through the process of pain and suffering primarily because you entered the arena under the wrong pretenses. You went forth because someone said you had a good ministry, or you sound good, or because people start giving you a title (prophet, apostle, etc.); however, you never sought God to find out if you truly are those things. You simply allowed what someone else said to convince you that this is what God has in mind for you, and now you're in that place, the place that God refers to in the book of Revelation 2:4 when he says: "Nevertheless I have *somewhat* against thee, because thou hast left thy first love."

What is that first love? Is that first love really leaving God, or leaving the assignment? The assignment that you were most passionate about; the assignment that really birthed life in you; it transformed and transcended you, the assignment that you can complete without thought. It is when you can operate it in the middle of the night without process or thinking or practicing. It is the assignment that you have left for something else that you're premature in. Because you're going for the title instead of the work, and so often people find themselves doing this…on a daily basis. And it's extremely prevalent in the church.

You see people who are Prophets yet are serving as a pastor. Here's the thing that I had to learn: You can be a pastor with the gift of prophecy, but it's impossible for you to be a prophet with the gift of pasturing except that God has called you to such assignment. This is because if you are a pastor, you can't do what a prophet would do. A prophet would call it like it is; a pastor must instill a level of wisdom, humility and thought on the process to determine the best approach. When the prophet comes in, there is no filter but as a pastor you must have a filter to some degree. And when you don't, you find yourself angry, frustrated, and suffocating, because you're stuck in the incubator of life.

You are depending on people to birth life into you. If they don't come to church, you don't know if you're going to have a good service. If they don't pay their tithes and offering, you don't know how the church will operate. Why? Because you're not experienced enough— you did not undergo a full-term birth, only a premature one. When you're premature, you can't handle the tasks at hand and its totality. You're constantly repeating the process because you're chasing what you think it's supposed to be. You're stuck in the incubator.

What's the incubator? It's the thing that helps you survive until you can become stable. But what happens if your stability was not designed by God for pastoring until 20 years in the future? You have wasted 20 years of your life trying to be something you will never reach until the term comes. When you could have been processing, changing, developing, fulfilling, being the wonder *God* called you to be in the current time so that in your latter years you would be prepared to walk in your appropriate calling. Because at that point you would have the knowledge and experience to draw from in order to increase that call and assignment that's upon your life, which is so important to developing the key of great discipline and discipleship. The Scriptures show that restoration is a valuable and essential endeavor, not only with the society and principles of the church in which I grew up. True restoration is vital to one's development as an individual; it properly prepares you for the next level. During my season of discovery, I came to the realization that to walk in restoration, I had to understand the sacrifice necessary to leave your past actions in the past. Consider what it means to be restored and how restoration is accomplished.

Oftentimes, we ask God to restore us, but we fail to realize that restoration is more than a few words of asking for forgiveness. It's a breakdown of one's life; it's getting past what you are accustomed to; it's changing atmospheres and surroundings; it's the power of forgiving others who have wronged you.

What does it mean to be restored?

We have been given an exhortation in Galatians 6:1: "Brethren if a man be overtaken in a fault, ye which are spiritual, restore such a one in the spirit of meekness; considering thyself, lest thou also be tempted."

Restore means to repair, fit, frame, or mend. This implies not only that the recipient of restoration is in some sort of disrepair or error, but that there is a pattern by which we must be framed or fitted. All humans are aware of their imperfections and everyone agrees that "no one is perfect." Since the beginning of time, God has given mankind a pattern, and men and women have always fallen short of this pattern. Romans 3:23 tells us, "For all have sin and come short of the glory of God." Restoration means that we are in a constant state of repairing our broken lives. It also requires us to be submissive to a power much higher than ourselves because it takes humility to recognize that there are things that need to be fixed.

This humility glorifies God because we gladly give Him the authority to dictate how we live our lives. When we find that we are living in a way or doing something more, less, or different than He has commanded, we recognize that we are the ones in error and must do the changing.

To make that change, we must go through the process of rehabilitation, which is not only the restoration of someone to a useful place in society, but also the analysis, examination, or investigation of someone. Romans 8:28-36 says:

> And we know that all things work together for good to them that love God, to them who are the called according to His purpose. For whom He did foreknow, He also did predestinate to be conformed to the image of His son, that he might be the firstborn among many brethren. Moreover, whom He did predestinate, them He also called: and whom He called, them He also justified: and whom He justified, them He also glorified. What shall we then say to these things? If God be for us, who can be against us? He that spared not his own son, but delivered him up for us all, how shall he not with him also freely give us all things? Who shall lay anything to the charge of God's elect? It is God that justifieth. Who is he that condemneth? It is Christ that died, yea rather, that is risen again, who is even at the right hand of God, who also maketh intercession for us. Who shall separate us from the love of Christ? Shall tribulation, or distress, or persecution, or famine, or nakedness, or peril, or sword? As it is written, for thy sake we are killed all day long; we are accounted as sheep for the slaughter.

When God restores us, He restores us completely. As written in 2 Corinthians 5:17, "Therefore, if any

man be in Christ, he is a new creature: old things are passed away; behold all things are made new." This process changes your level of faith and trust in God. I always say that "faith is only as strong as the test it succeeds in life."

~Carey L. Gidron Sr.~

In this season of my faith-walk, I have had to learn how to appreciate what God has been doing in my life with new relationships, friendships, and partnerships. I've found myself not thinking that which seemed to be strange. I knew God was still in control of my destiny. I knew that He would not allow people who had the wrong agenda to connect with me, to latch hold of my life, and stay long.

He has been faithfully cutting those relationships off on the short side of time. Before, they would have been connected for years only to devastate my future and destroy my end. Many times, in ministry, I have found myself alone and I prayed that God would give me true friends who would be there for me. Despite my disappointments, I never lost faith in God.

There's something unique about being a go-getter. But what's more unique is knowing why you were created, why you were born, and understanding that YOU are born with ambition. And no one can give it or take it away. There are those who watch things happen, those who wish things would happen, and those who make things happen. I had to discover which one I was. I had to determine whether I was a dreamer, a wisher, or a creator of things to happen. It's an amazing thing to know someone you love is happy, but it's another thing when you get up and create your own happiness.

During my season of betrayal, I got mad at everyone—even God—just to discover that God was not in negotiation mode over or regarding my condition, situation, or circumstances. He doesn't have to argue with me about my situation or its outcome. If we believe Him as we confess, then we are required to take Him at His word. He is not confused at any level. It is us who must activate our faith to gain access to a faithful God.

You may experience the pains of life and feel like disconnecting and withdrawing. However, this is not the time to shelter your emotions and live life alone. Be willing to pray to God. Remember, He knows, but talking to Him grants Him the permission to intervene. Never give up on God. Boldly go before His presence—take on the tenacity to move forward!

I found out a long time ago that to be a follower of Christ it is essential to relinquish ties with people who don't follow in the same direction. I learned that I may not always fit in, or always be liked, be accepted. But the one thing that I am assured of is that my isolation from man is worth the love of God and the relationship that I have with Him now.

CHAPTER 8

GET A FRESH START

When letting go of people, places, and things, we may struggle, wondering if we will ever find peace and happiness in the new. We can get sucked into staying in the wrong assignment in life out of duty or fear that nothing better will ever come along. Some believers truly believe that being connected to the wrong leadership or relationship is better than being alone. Feeling desperate is never a good recipe for a relationship. When a relationship or assignment takes away one's joy and laughter in life, it may be time to say goodbye and mean it; don't keep renewing what has died. The book of Ecclesiastes talks about seasons. To everything there is a season, and a time for every assignment under heaven. There is a time to gain, and a time to lose; a time to keep and a time to throw away.

There is no reason to feel bad when we outgrow some relationships. To hang on to something that is no longer working for you is silly. Get the anointing of removal. Start today while reading this book, removing names and numbers from the speed dial on your phones or from your e-mail and social media. Your season of betrayal is over; let's take a closer step toward liberation. All is not lost when it is time to move on. We can value the lessons learned from friends even when the friendships are no longer active or meaningful.

New life, dream, goals, and visions have emerged, and it is time to get rid of the clutter. As you grow into your new season of promotion, lose the propensity to want to hold on to old things. Drop the excuses, stop thinking you need these old relationships that continue to contaminate your life; I say if it has not made a difference in all this time, what difference will it make now? We hold on to past betrayal convincing ourselves that one day things will turn in our favor, finding great comfort in it; but no, more!!! betrayal can deter you from getting what God has promised for your life, and it can become burdensome to manage. We must trust God and his word to keep us safe and protected as we now move forward.

Deuteronomy15:1 says: "At the end of every seven years you must cancel the debts of everyone who owes." Well, I have good news for you; this is your year of great release. Embrace it, love it, celebrate it....

Hear me well: When people decide to walk out of your life, let them get to stepping! Give them an official dismissal. Tell them please raise your hand and repeat after me, "May the LORD watch between you and me when we are absent one from the other" (Genesis 31:49).

Functioning in the Right Call is extremely important. During your season of promotion, distractions are unaccepted!

– Carey Gidron, Sr.

There are times when you may ask yourself, "Am I fulfilling God's perfect plan?" You know the Scripture you must believe that God will give you your every expectation as it pertains to reaching and accomplishing your life's goals and dreams. But what if you have not received the results that you have been expecting? I recommend that you reflect on the Word in Philippians 1:6 says, "Being confident of this very thing, that he which hath begun a good work in you will perform it until the day of Jesus Christ." Keep this in your mind. Hold fast to it in your heart. Understand that you are not a mistake. You were created for a reason. You are here on purpose and you are great because God has called you by name.

You were created to be free. Galatians 5:1 teaches, "Stand fast therefore in liberty wherewith Christ has made us free and be not entangled again with the yoke of bondage." Remind yourself that you were created with a purpose; created with a plan; created to be free. You must understand that every failure brings you a step closer to kingdom progression, because you are now able to use your experiences from the lessons learned. This concept brings you into a truth that sets you free from the backlash of failed dreams, visions, goals, and plans whether in your ministry, family, personal, or professional life. You will know when you are free when a great peace comes over you and the very thoughts and opinions of others have no more influence over your ability to succeed.

The most important lesson I desire you to take away from your journey with me is this: When you obey God, you can expect the unexpected to happen when you move forward. In God's plan and vision, there is only one way to move in the Kingdom...and that's forward. When we move forward, the Lord will open the door!

You have to hit the ropes to bounce back. Make your opponent feel as if you wanted to hit them. Winning is defined as the result of a competition or contest that results in a victory. Winning satisfies the extrinsic motivation of your being, but it is determined based upon someone else's viewpoint. The referee is the judge in a boxing match or competition, and they have the assignment of reviewing any faults, mistakes, or mishaps in the match to determine who the true winner is.

Even when there is a time of extreme gore, hurt, and pain toward a competitor, the referee has the permission to step in and pull the competitor off from harming the opponent any further.

In life, we face many adversities, tests, trials, and tribulations. We find ourselves in boxing rings: rings of divorce, sickness, disease, hurt, and pain. In the rings of life, it feels like we can't take any more of the jabs, crosses, hooks, and uppercuts in our natural and spiritual lives. The blows to the face try to disable our ability to continue in the fight.

But before any extreme danger—such as broken spirits, injured prayer lives, and deformed faith—can happen, our referee steps in to pull our enemy off from us.

Bonus Section!!: Winning Outside of the Ring

Psalms 35 *Plead my cause, O LORD, with them that strive with me: fight against them that fight against me.*

In the battle you're in, you must act aggressive. Anytime you're met with a physical altercation, your opponent gets in your face, talking stuff to provoke you to throw the first punch. They try to sow further discord into the situation. The purpose of getting in your face is to belittle who you are in front of onlookers, or to scare you even further. But sometimes instead of showing fear, running away, and fretting you must show aggression back. Even if you can't fight, you must be bold enough to show your enemy you are not afraid of them.

Even in your spirituality you can't show fear when the enemy attacks you; you can't allow his tactics to belittle you or your faith in God. You must learn how to show aggression to the enemy, why? Because often times, the reason we get beat upside the head is because we operate in our flesh. You must show aggression by having a dangerous prayer life and a dangerous faith in God. Stop coming to the enemy with uppercuts and jabs in the natural, but uppercut and jab him in the spirit. That's why the Bible teaches in 2Corinthians 10:4, "For the weapons of our warfare are not carnal, but mighty through God to the pulling down of strong holds."

We can no longer approach the enemy in our second creation, which is flesh, but we must approach him in our first creation. In your first creation, you see God; that's why Scriptures teach in Romans 8:17, "And if children, then heirs; heirs of God, and joint-heirs with Christ; if so be that we suffer with him, that we may be also glorified together." So if he wins, you win. But you can't win without the correct and appropriate attire; therefore you must put on the whole armor of God.

You Have to Hit the Ropes and Bounce Back

The ropes of the ring are a powerful thing, and a necessary component to the success of your match. The ropes can bless you, but they also have the unknown ability to deceive your enemy. Many believe the ropes and posts of the ring are the most hopeless and vulnerable places of the ring. When your opponent pins you against the rope, they believe you are powerless.

In life, the enemy pushes us against the ropes of our rings and tries to render us powerless. In this point and time, we have the very little mobility in the corner of the ring; we can't lift our arms or our legs to dash underneath our opponent to get to a safe zone.

The enemy has you pinned up in the corner and you are unable to get free. The only mobility you have is the mobility of your head, which is key to winning your match. Your eyes enable you to see past where you are; your eyes signal help. That's why the Bible says, "I will lift mine eyes to the hills whence cometh my help." For all my help comes from the Lord….Remember God is on your side and with him you win..Amen.